> Dear Sherri,
>
> I pray that yo[u] which God has called you! May God richly bless you as you continue to serve Him!
>
> Pastor Matt
> Prov. 11:30

Dynamic Devotions

Volume 1

Dynamic Devotions

Volume 1

Mike Sanders

XULON PRESS

Xulon Press
2301 Lucien Way #415
Maitland, FL 32751
407.339.4217
www.xulonpress.com

© 2020 by Mike Sanders

All rights reserved solely by the author. The author guarantees all contents are original and do not infringe upon the legal rights of any other person or work. No part of this book may be reproduced in any form without the permission of the author. The views expressed in this book are not necessarily those of the publisher.

Unless otherwise indicated, Scripture quotations taken from the King James Version (KJV) – *public domain*.

Scripture quotations taken from the New King James Version (NKJV). Copyright © 1982 by Thomas Nelson, Inc. Used by permission. All rights reserved.

Scripture quotations taken from the English Standard Version (ESV). Copyright © 2001 by Crossway, a publishing ministry of Good News Publishers. Used by permission. All rights reserved.

Paperback ISBN-13: 978-1-6312-9975-9
Ebook ISBN-13: 978-1-6312-9976-6

This book is dedicated to my amazing wife, Terri Sanders, who has ministered with me for thirty years. I am so thankful for the dedication she has shown to Christ and His Church. Thank you for making a difference. You're appreciated so much. "Be steadfast, immovable, always abounding in the work of the Lord, knowing that in the Lord your labor is not in vain." 1 Corinthians 15:58.

Table of Contents

Foreword ix

A Passion for Good Works 1
Celebrating the Lord's Supper 3
Dealing with Life's Gray Areas 7
How to Demonstrate Humility in Our Lives 11
How to Find Our Place in the Church 15
Finding Our Identity in Christ! 17
How to Respond to Tragedy 19
He Gives More Grace 23
Dealing with Spiritual Intimidation 25
Overcoming Materialism 29
The Centrality of the Cross 31
The Danger of Sin in Our Lives 35
The Marks of a Mature Christian 37
Three Guidelines on Making Judgments 41
Four Keys to Effective Evangelism and Missions through
the Church 45
Faithfulness 47
Be a Peacemaker Not a Troublemaker 49
Patient in Trials & Temptations 53
The Mission of the Church 57
About the Author 59

Foreword

Life is a journey. It is a path that we are on and there are some helps we need along the way. One of those helps is time alone with God. In your hand is a very helpful book that will aid you on your journey as you listen to God speak to your heart.

A devotional book is designed for individuals to read for their personal edification and formation. I am delighted my dear friend, Pastor Mike Sanders, has written this one. Mike pastors The Open Door Church of Chambersburg, Pennsylvania. This church is my favorite because I spent twenty-five years ministering there as her pastor (1970-1995), and I am delighted Mike leads the ministry there now. Mike has a passion for God's Word and is daily in the Bible for his own study and edification. All pastors need to study for preparation of their sermons and other speeches, but it is necessary for all Christians, especially pastors who shepherd others, to be in God's Word for their own spiritual growth. On these pages you will find words written by a faithful pastor gleaned from his own personal time of meditation, reflection, and spiritual instruction from God. These words are encouraging, enlightening, and edifying to help you through your journey of life.

Jesus Himself often spent time alone with His Heavenly Father. He would withdraw from daily activities, demands of the ministry, and the constant barrage of questions from followers to spend time alone with His Father. This priority of silence is found on many of the pages of the gospel accounts.

Jesus is an example to us on how He prepared for important events. His high priestly prayer in John 17 prepared the Son of God's most important event to go to the cross. If you desire to go deeper with Jesus then time alone with God is a necessity. I am often reminded of the man identified as the Ethiopian who asked Philip, the evangelist, to guide him with what he was reading from the prophet Isaiah (Acts 8). Someone needed to guide him. Philip guided him right to Jesus. As you take this devotional book while carefully and prayerfully reading the words you will have someone who has spent time with God helping you. So read the pages deliberately and you will learn, but more importantly, you will be touched in your spirit of the greatness of our Lord Jesus Christ.

Thank you, Pastor Mike Sanders, for helping us on our spiritual journey.

Dino J. Pedrone
Founder and President of DPMinistries

A Passion for Good Works

Titus 2:11-14

At the heart of Christianity is the truth that we are forgiven and accepted by God, not because of what we have done but because of what He has done. Christ forgives not because we deserve it, but out of His sheer love and grace. "[Christ] hath saved us, and called us with an holy calling, not according to our works, but according to his own purpose and grace, which was given us in Christ Jesus before the world began" (2 Tim. 1:9 KJV). Someone aptly defined grace as an acronym: GRACE is *G*od's *R*iches *A*t *C*hrist's *E*xpense[1]

We know that Christ has completed the work of salvation, yet the work of sanctification goes on. God's grace is powerful and transforms a person (Eph. 2:8-10). God's grace shapes our thinking and living. We must see faith evident in our lives and work. The Bible says that after God saves us, He creates us to serve.

God's grace is a conquering grace. God has promised us victory over sin. Someone who looks at grace as a license to sin has missed grace entirely. "God is able to make all grace abound toward you, that you, always having all sufficiency in all things,

---

[1] John F. MacArthur Jr., The Gospel according to the Apostles: The Role of Works in the Life of Faith (Nashville, TN: Word Pub., 2000).

may have an abundance for every good work" (2 Cor. 9:8 NKJV). Grace empowers us to renounce ungodliness (Rom. 6:1-4).

Why should anyone believe Christianity? Where do we find its credibility? People want to know, "Is this Christian message credible?" In our culture, can anyone believe anything that anybody says? So why should anyone believe a Christian? Why should anyone believe the gospel in our world today? Well, there is one irrefutable argument. The proof of the pudding is in the eating. If this Good News transforms people's lives—if "liars, evil beasts, and lazy gluttons" (Tit. 1:12) became self-controlled, upright, holy, and disciplined people (Tit. 1:8)—then the credibility of the message will be secured. Moreover, that is the function of the Gospel of Grace. Grace gives us the power that enables our obedience to Christ.

Good deeds are not the foundation of our salvation but the fruit. "That the man of God may be competent, equipped for every good work" (2 Tim. 3:17 ESV). Do your best for God. The highest prize that any person could receive is from the lips of Jesus Himself, when He says to you, "Well done, thou good and faithful servant: thou hast been faithful over a few things, I will make thee ruler over many things: enter thou into the joy of thy lord" (Matt. 25:21, 23 KJV). The happiest people are those who are using whatever they have for the glory of God right now.

Celebrating the Lord's Supper

1 Corinthians 11:17-34

The universal practice and pattern of the Church has been to observe the Lord's Supper. "And they continued stedfastly in the apostles' doctrine and fellowship, and in breaking of bread, and in prayers" (Acts 2:42 KJV). The Lord's supper is the last supper that Jesus dined with His apostles before He was forsaken and crucified, as a sacrificial death for our sins. Jesus transformed the Jewish Passover celebration into a symbol of far greater significance.

It was at this meal He instituted the ordinance of the Lord's Supper to be followed by Christians, during which we are to commemorate His death. It is a memorial service: *"This do ye, as oft as ye drink it, in remembrance of me"* (1 Cor. 11:25). You will find the phrase *"this do in remembrance of Me"* in both **vv.24,25.** The verb *'do'* is continuous in the original language and signifies a command to continue *'doing'* what He has said we should do *'in remembrance of Him.'*

The Lord's Supper is an object lesson that represents a great spiritual truth for believers. As we celebrate the Lord's Supper, we need to remember Christ has forgiven our sins. It is only through Christ that He delivers us from judgment, and we experience forgiveness of sins and eternal life in heaven with God. When we partake of the Lord's Supper, we are entering into communion with Christ. "The cup of blessing, which we bless, is it not the communion of the blood of Christ? The bread which we break is it not the communion of the body of Christ?" (1 Cor. 10:16 KJV).

Communion should not be entered into lightly by anyone, especially by those who participate. The apostle Paul says concerning the Lord's Supper, 'Examine yourself.' This ordinance involves a self-examination of any who participate. As believers, we are to examine ourselves before we partake of the Lord's Supper. Only those who are in a right relationship with the Lord are to participate.

According to the Associated Press, on the evening of February 6, 1996, three friends drove the rural roads of east Tampa, Florida, with the intent of playing a prank. Tragically, their game was anything but funny. They pulled some twenty street signs out of the ground, including the stop sign at one fatal intersection.

The next day, three eighteen-year-old buddies, who had just finished bowling, breezed through that intersection without stopping. Their car sailed into the path of an eight-ton truck, and they were all killed.

One year later, the three perpetrators of the deadly prank were convicted of manslaughter. In June of 1997, they stood in orange jail jumpsuits and handcuffs before a judge in a Tampa courtroom, weeping and wiping their eyes, as they were sentenced to fifteen years in prison.

It is a dangerous thing, with tragic consequences, for anyone to take down signposts on highways. It is no less hazardous for anyone to vandalize the signpost that God puts on the road of life. When we honor God's commandment, we point the way to the signposts of life. If we dishonor God's commandments, we can unwittingly lead others to destruction. This is a time for us to examine ourselves. Paul said that if we judge ourselves, we shall not fall under God's judgment of this sin of taking communion in an unworthy manner.

Dealing with Life's Gray Areas

> "Food will not commend us to God. We are no worse off if we do not eat, and no better off if we do. But take care that this right of yours does not somehow become a stumbling block to the weak"
> (1 Cor. 8:8-9 ESV).

One fact that we will quickly find among Christians is that not everyone agrees on everything. Unfortunately, there are church splits because of the color of the carpet in the sanctuary. However, along those lines, not all Christians agree on what is right and what is wrong. For one, the questionable matter may be black and white, and to another, it may be gray. One may feel that a person should not go to a specific place, whereas another sees nothing wrong with it. One may think that doing a particular thing is wrong, while another sees nothing wrong with it.

What is right? What is wrong? How far does Christian freedom go regarding discretionary behavior not explicitly forbidden in Scripture? Many practices are not commanded, commended, or prohibited in Scripture. They are neither black nor white, but gray. Such issues in one age or area may not be the same as those in other times or places, but every age and every Christian must deal with the gray areas of Christian living.

1 Corinthians chapters 8-10 deal with the church's questions regarding meat offered to idols. The Greeks sacrificed animals to their gods. They served the meat at large cafeterias near

the temple—and much of it made its way to the food market. So, when people went down to Food Lion to pick up a T-bone, chances are they had offered that meat to an idol.

Many Corinthian disciples had no problem with eating meat that was handled at a pagan temple. The meat was neither clean nor unclean to many. [Christians] argued that since idols were "nothing," they were free to eat the meat.[2]

Through this debate in the early Church, the apostle Paul presents to us four questions that will assist us in making the right decisions about gray areas.

Will we become spiritually prideful?

> "Knowledge puffs up, but love edifies. And if anyone thinks that he knows anything, he knows nothing yet as he ought to know" (*1 Cor. 8:1-2 NKJV*).

Knowledge without love corrupts us. We must be careful that we do not develop a prideful and arrogant attitude toward others on the gray issues. Just because a certain matter does not bother our conscience does not mean that we are better than others. People are in different places on their journey of faith. As a result, this requires us to be understanding and considerate of others.

Will we cause someone else to stumble?

> "But take care that this liberty of yours does not somehow become a stumbling block to the weak" (1 Cor. 8:9 NASB).

---

[2] Thomas Nelson, I. (1995). The Woman's Study Bible (1 Co 8:1). Nashville: Thomas Nelson.

As mature believers our calling is to think about others and not just ourselves. Because God uses our conscience to guide us, we should respect the consciences of other believers as well. In the name of Christian freedom, many believers have been spiritually misled and hurt. We should cautiously use our freedom in Christ and remember other believers who need guidance. "Let each of you look not only to his own interests, but also to the interests of others" (Phil 2:4 ESV).

The late Dawson Trotman, the founder of The Navigators, was visiting Taiwan on one of his overseas trips. During the visit, he hiked with a Taiwanese pastor back into one of the mountain villages to meet with some of the national Christians. The roads and trails were wet, and their shoes became very muddy. Later, someone asked this Taiwanese pastor what he remembered most about Dawson Trotman. Without hesitation, the man replied, "He cleaned my shoes."

How surprised this humble national pastor must have been to arise in the morning and realize that the Christian leader from America had risen before him and cleaned the mud from his shoes. Dawson Trotman, throughout his Christian life, had a spirit of servanthood. He died as he lived, actually giving his life to rescue someone else from drowning.[3]

Are we setting the right example for others?

"For if anyone sees you who have knowledge eating in an idol's temple, will not the conscience of him who is weak be emboldened to eat those things offered to idols?"
(1 Cor. 8:10 NKJV).

---

[3] Barry L. Davis, *52 Sermons from the Gospel of John*, Pulpit Outlines Series (knap.: Barry Davis, 2013), 84.

Everyone influences someone! We live in a world that needs people to be good examples. We should not shy away from offering ourselves as an ethical model for believers. "For you, yourselves know how you ought to imitate us because we were not idle when we were with you" (2 Thess. 3:7 ESV). God always wraps His truth in a person.

Are we building others up in their faith?

"And so by your knowledge this weak person is destroyed, the brother for whom Christ died"
(1 Cor. 8:11 ESV).

Unfortunately, the vocabulary of Christians is often void of terms such as build up, strengthen, and edify. As believers, we should be helping our brothers and sisters in Christ. We have a greater responsibility to help other followers of Christ to grow in their faith. It should be our desire to live a life that lifts others, not carelessly pulls others down. "All things are lawful," but not all things are helpful. "All things are lawful," but not all things build up" (1 Cor. 10:23 ESV).

How to Demonstrate Humility in Our Lives

1 Corinthians 4:6-13

In *Mere Christianity,* C. S. Lewis writes,

> There is one vice of which no man in the world is free; which everyone in the world loathes when he sees it in someone else; and of which hardly any people, except Christians, ever imagine that they are guilty themselves. I have heard people admit that they are bad-tempered, or that they cannot keep their heads about girls or drink, or even that they are cowards. I do not think I have ever heard anyone who was not a Christian accuse himself of this vice. And at the same time, I have very seldom met anyone, who was not a Christian, who showed the slightest mercy to it in others. There is no fault which makes a man more unpopular, and no fault which we are more unconscious of in ourselves. And the more we have it ourselves, the more we dislike it in others.... The vice I am talking of is Pride or

Self-Conceit. Pride leads to every other vice: it is the complete anti-God state of mind.[4]

The Corinthian Christians had not learned the virtue of humility in their life. Therefore, the apostle stressed, "...that none of you may be puffed up on behalf of one against the other" (1 Cor. 4:6 NKJV). The place of humility is a place of blessing and joy. Self-absorbed, arrogant people who live life with a "what's in it for me" attitude are not happy people. Happy people are those who've learned to give of themselves to others. Happiness starts with humility.

Christianity would benefit significantly if there were more humble individuals in both pulpits and pews. Many of us could use a bit more humility. So let us pause and pray that God would use His Word to build true humility in our lives.

We must begin by addressing conceit in our lives. We do this by keeping perspective of our role in God's kingdom. We are all servants and stewards for Christ. "Serving the Lord with all humility of mind" (Acts 20:19 KJV). We minister for the Glory of God. As servants, we must do His will without regard of our desires.

Never take credit for what God has done in your life. Mark Twain said, "It is amazing what can be done if no one minds who gets the credit." We are like the moon reflecting the light of the sun. Redirect any personal praise to Christ.

Pride is out of sync with God. *"For if a man think himself to be something when he is nothing, he deceiveth himself"* (*Gal. 6:3 KJV*). Don't let pride keep you away from the altar. Repent if you have sin in your life; don't be concerned about what others will think. We should never think that we are better than anyone

---

[4] T. J. Betts, *Amos: An Ordinary Man with an Extraordinary Message*, Focus on the Bible Commentary (Ross-shire, Scotland: Christian Focus, 2011), 121.

else. Unity in our relationships can come only from an attitude of genuine humility. "Clothe yourselves, all of you, with humility toward one another, for 'God opposes the proud but gives grace to the humble'" (1 Pet. 5:5 ESV).

We have no grounds for pride or boasting in ourselves. That is the point that the apostle Paul wanted to make to the Corinthians. "For who makes you differ from another? And what do you have that you did not receive? Now, if you did indeed receive it, why do you boast as if you had not received it?" (1 Cor. 4:7 NKJV).

We learn that there are three great questions to ask ourselves. Who regards us as superior? What do we have that we did not receive? Why do we boast as if we did not receive it? Just as pride is the root of all sin, so humility is the root of all righteousness. "Humble yourselves therefore under the mighty hand of God, that he may exalt you in due time" (1 Pet. 5:6 KJV).

Christ humbled Himself when He came into this world, as is taught in *Philippians 2:6-8. Humility was the principal characteristic of the life of Christ.*[5] May He be our example.

Albert Pujols, the first baseman for the St. Louis Cardinals, is a World Series champ, an eight-time All-Star, the recipient of three National League MVP awards, and according to a 2008 poll of thirty MLB managers, the most feared hitter in the sport. Even more impressive is his life off the field. The Pujols Family Foundation he started offers support and care to people with Down syndrome and their families, while also helping the poor in the Dominican Republic. He and his wife of ten years provide a loving household for four little children. But most importantly, he is a passionate disciple of Christ.

---

[5] Crawford, C. C. (1919). Sermon Outlines on Acts (p. 65). Cincinnati, OH: Standard.

While speaking at an event at Lafayette Senior High School in Missouri, Pujols told the audience of men and young boys, "As a Christian, our calling is to live a holy life. My standard for living is set by God, not by the world. I am responsible for growing and sharing the gospel." Then, after reading Paul's words in Philippians 2:3, "Do nothing out of selfish ambition or vain conceit, but in humility consider others better than yourselves"—Pujols told the crowd, "One way for me to stay satisfied in Jesus is for me to stay humble. Humility is getting on your knees and staying in God's will—what He wants for me, not what the world wants." He added: "It would be easy to go out and do whatever I want, but those things only satisfy the flesh for a moment. Jesus satisfies my soul forever."[6]

---

[6] Barry L. Davis, *52 Sermons about Jesus*, Pulpit Outlines Series (Barry Davis, 2012), 20.

How to Find Our Place in the Church

1 Corinthians 12:1-31

The apostle Paul teaches us to be informed about our spiritual gifts. "Now concerning spiritual gifts, brethren, I would not have you ignorant" (1 Cor. 12:1 KJV). Only believers have spiritual gifts, and every Christian is gifted. "But to each one of us, grace was given according to the measure of Christ's gift" (Eph. 4:7 NKJV). Spiritual gifts are divine tools to accomplish eternal results. A spiritual gift is a primary channel by which the Holy Spirit can minister through the believer.

There are three categories of spiritual gifts: Sign Gifts, Speaking Gifts, Serving Gifts. The four significant lists of spiritual gifts are in Romans 12:3-8; 1 Corinthians 12:1-11; Ephesians 4:11-12; 1 Peter 4:10-11. Each list gives examples of spiritual gifts, and these gifts are vital for Christian ministry.

> You can learn a skill,
> You can acquire a talent,
> But you are given a gift.

John MacArthur writes, "No local congregation will be what it should be...until it understands spiritual gifts" ("The Church," page 136). Therefore, we should be discerning about spiritual gifts. We must realize that there are different gifts, ministries, and results. Don't envy someone else's gift. Every member has a different function. Identify your spiritual gifts, focus on one purpose, and match your gifts with ministry.

God didn't put us on this earth to live for ourselves. Every member is a minister in the body of Christ. We should minister to others through our spiritual gifts. "As every man hath received the gift, even so, minister the same one to another, as good stewards of the manifold grace of God" (1 Pet. 4:10 KJV). A spiritual gift is a blessing and should bring glory to Christ. God granted me a gift, not for me but for you. God assigned you a gift, not for you but for me. If you do not use your gift, you are depriving me; if I don't use my gift, I am depriving you.

As believers, we are one body and one team. When everyone on the team is engaged in ministry, everyone benefits. "A Christian who does not have a ministry is a contradiction of terms" (John MacArthur). Jesus came to minister to others for His Father. His spirit gives gifts to His people so that they can do the same.

Remember, every gift is essential. Spiritual gifts are not for entertainment or our boasting. God gives us spiritual gifts to build us up so that we can grow into the image of Christ. God has given each of His followers supernatural abilities to empower, encourage, and help one another. There is always someone to help. There is always someone to serve.

Finding Our Identity in Christ!

Colossians 2:10-15

As we strive to find our identity in Christ, remember our identity used to be in the world, but now as believers and as a result of our salvation in Christ, our identity is rooted in Jesus. We have been granted a new status in Christ. So many people today, even believers, find their identity in their job, their children, or in money, whether they have it or not. They find their identity in who likes them and who doesn't. They find their identity in their past or current relationships. I am not saying that any or all of these things are bad or evil. What I am saying is that if these things are the root and foundation of your life, then you are going to crash and burn. All of these things are temporary; these things come and go.

It is so essential, in the Christian life, that we understand that our foundation is in Christ. Our identity is in Jesus. Being a Christian involves a radical change of character. We do not relate or identify ourselves with the world or the things of the world, but instead, we identify ourselves with Christ and Christ alone. In Christ, we have a new identity that results in a new set of values in our minds and hearts. It results in a new direction in our lives. It results in a new set of ethics that are rooted in the Scriptures that we live by, and thus we find our identity in Christ.

When we come to Colossians 2:10-15, the false teachers have already permeated the church at Colossae and were causing doubt in the hearts and minds of the followers of Christ. The apostle writes this letter to remind the believers of the foundation that they have in Jesus Christ. He tells them that they do not have to search for something better or something else for their faith and walk with God. All that they have ever needed is found in Christ.

In verse 10, note what the scripture says: "You are complete in him." I would encourage you to mark that in your Bible because you will keep coming back to this verse. Day by day the devil beats on us and tries to persuade us to believe that we are not complete in Christ. He wants us to believe that somehow our relationship with Christ is insufficient and that we need to find something else to make us whole; to give us meaning and purpose in life. The apostle tells us, right out of the gate, in verse 10, that you are complete in Him. He is referring to Christ, which is the head of all principality and power.

That's what I want you to walk away with today. I want you to know the confidence of who you are in Jesus Christ as a believer. If you don't know Christ, I want you to come to Christ today. Come to the cross and find Jesus Christ as your Lord and Savior. Jesus arose from the dead and is still alive, still seeking souls, and He wants to enter your heart today. Know who you are and quit playing the silly games of the world and trying to figure out who you are. The Bible tells us who we are in Christ. It means to be made whole. You are made full in Christ.

How to Respond to Tragedy

Luke 13:1-5

It seems like every day we encounter tragedies from all parts of the world. Everywhere we turn, we hear about life's adversities. Because of technology, it does not isolate us from calamities.

When tragedies strike, who is responsible? Some people blame governments, some people blame guns, some people blame God, and some people blame the victims for their sin. So, who is to blame? Jesus addressed these questions that will help us sort out this issue.

"There were present at that season some who told Him about the Galileans whose blood Pilate had mingled with their sacrifices" (Luke 13:1 NKJV). Pilate, the Roman governor of Judaea, discovered a plot by the Galilean pilgrims, to attack the Roman authorities. As a result, the Galileans were massacred by Pilate as they were sacrificing in the temple at Jerusalem.

Many people in the ancient world, and even today, believe that a person's suffering is directly proportionate to their sin.[7] "And his disciples asked him, saying, Master, who did sin, this man, or his parents, that he was born blind?" (John 9:2 KJV).

---

[7] Sproul, R. C. (1999). *A Walk with God: An Exposition of Luke* (p. 276). Great Britain: Christian Focus Publications.

In this passage, Jesus teaches us that not all suffering is a judgment of Heaven. "Jesus answered and said to them, Do you suppose that these Galileans were worse sinners than all *other* Galileans because they suffered such things?" **(Luke 13:2 NKJV)**.

The three crucial issues of life are these: the problem of suffering, the effect of death, and the subject of eternity. Tragedy can strike any of us at any moment. The question is not why innocent people suffer, but why didn't we suffer.

Hell is life's greatest tragedy. Prepare your hearts and make sure that you are ready to meet Jesus Christ. Who knows what a day may bring forth? Turn from your sin and receive Christ as your Savior! We all deserve judgment for our sin, but Christ took that judgment on the cross for us. God will welcome us with open arms if we repent and receive His forgiveness.

Reach out to those in need. Jesus said, "As ye go, preach, saying, The kingdom of heaven is at hand" (Matt. 10:7 KJV). People today are searching for hope amid personal despair and tragedy. The world knows only of dying hope. The Bible says, "Such are the paths of all who forget God; the hope of the godless shall perish" (Job 8:13 ESV). In contrast, believers in Christ have a living hope. The Prophet Jeremiah reminds us, "For I know the plans I have for you, declares the LORD, plans for welfare and not for evil, to give you a future and a hope" (Jer. 29:11 ESV).

Start conversations with others about suffering and tragedy and lead people to the hope we have in Christ. Emphasize that tragedy reminds us to have our spiritual house in order.

"The gospel is not that Jesus Christ comes to earth, tells us how to live, we live a good life, and then God owes us a blessing. The gospel is that Jesus Christ came to earth, lived the life we should have lived and died the death we should have died" (Tim Keller).

Remember what is essential. We can glorify God in our suffering. God can use dark and stressful times for our good. He will use them to teach you to trust Him: "We stopped relying on ourselves and learned to rely only on God" (2 Cor. 8-9).

How grateful we should be for those influential and unique people who have made positive impressions upon us. What matters most is our faith in Christ and our family.

He Gives More Grace

James 4:6

I feel like this is a message that Christians need to hear more of. There may be times in our lives that we do not fully understand the great need of grace. As believers, we grasp that we need saving grace in our lives when we come to Christ and receive Him as our Savior.

We respond to the gospel in full submission, acknowledging our sinfulness and declaring that Christ is the one who died for our sins and trusting in Him alone for salvation. Too many Christians stop right there when it comes to grace. They do not recognize that God calls us to have mercy and that He gives us more grace. Grace upon grace He gives to the child of God.

He gives a sustaining grace, He gives a strengthening grace, He gives us speaking grace, and all through the Scriptures, we see that God gives us serving grace. We are in desperate need of the grace of God moment by moment in our Christian life. The question is, how is it that God imparts this grace to us?

God has not only ordained His message, but He has ordained His means or His methods by which He dispenses grace to not only those who do not know Christ but also those who do know Christ. Believers need to be careful. There is this idea creeping into the body of Christ that we do not need the means of grace but that it can be attained and received through the methods of the world.

How is it that God imparts grace to us? He gives it through His Word; He imparts it through prayer. He imparts it to us personally but also corporately. The peace of God is shed upon your life even as you gather corporately into the family of God.

The Hebrew writer continues to implore the Church not to forsake the assembling of yourselves together, and he says so much the more as you see the Day approaching. Do you think we're very close to the rapture of the Church and the coming of our Lord and Savior? I do, and so the answer is not to meet less; the answer is to meet more as God imparts grace.

Every time you come to the house of God to worship Him, praise Him, read His Word, and pray together as a family, He is infusing grace into your life. When you leave the gathering, you have that grace that sustains you and strengthens you that you might not only be faithful to God but serve Him joyfully.

God infuses His sustaining grace into your heart and your life through the means of the ordinances of the Church. Through baptism and communion God strengthens us. The ordinances of the Church do not save us, but they certainly bring us back to the message of the cross. Therefore, never undervalue the opportunity to come together as the people of God.

Take advantage of every opportunity that you have as a believer to gather with God's people. We, as believers, must recognize that God imparts His grace to us. There is no doubt that, even in the smallest group of believers, God is infusing His grace within our hearts and igniting faith within us.

Dealing with Spiritual Intimidation

Colossians 2:16-23

You're probably familiar with the HGTV show called *Fixer Upper,* starring Chip and Joanna Gaines. This husband-and-wife team work together to remodel and redesign homes that are in desperate need of repair. There are two reasons I dislike this show. First, it costs me money. Every time my wife watches this show, she gets ideas and begins thinking of things that we could do to our house! I tell her how she needs to be content and be happy with what she has. She then comes right back at me and says, "Why do we have to build new buildings at the church? Why aren't you happy and content?" She stops me in my tracks!

The second reason is I'm not a fixer-upper guy. I don't like to change a lot of lightbulbs. I try to drop a few to keep expectations low. This Chip guy, he's perfect, and he can fix anything for his wife, and he makes everything beautiful. Here's old Mike... he can't even change a lightbulb. He affects me deeply.

The reason I want to share that story is not to tell you my woes but to let you know that not too long ago, Chip and Joanna Gaines were in the news. There was a group of people who were upset at Chip and Joanna because their pastor had preached about real godly marriage. He stood up against same-sex marriage. He took a firm stand.

I found it ironic that the media and different groups were trying to intimidate Chip and Joanna as well as HGTV. These groups wanted them off the air because they didn't think or believe like them. This produced incredible pressure on HGTV. I appreciate Chip and Joanna because they didn't back down but stood firm on what they believed. Their pastor also stood firm and didn't back down.

This made me think a lot about intimidation, spiritual intimidation within the body of Christ and within the family of God. Many people try to intimidate God's people spiritually. To make God's people feel inferior because maybe you don't do it exactly as they do. When the apostle Paul writes this letter, he is addressing the Colossians as believers about making sure that they are not spiritually intimidated by false teachers who had infiltrated the church.

Paul gives a severe warning to all of us. The apostle takes time to remind us of the danger of being deceived and the danger of shifting from the whole of the gospel of Jesus Christ. The risk of forgetting what it means to be complete in Christ.

The Bible reminds us that we are complete in Christ and that completeness in Christ brings about a focus on our lives. An identity and purpose for our lives. The Scripture teaches us that Christ is the head of all principality and all power. There is no authority that is higher than Jesus Christ. We are followers of Christ. We do not follow the rules of a legalist. We do not buy into the conventional systems that compromise religious people, but instead, we support our Lord and Savior Jesus Christ. We have a living relationship with Him.

Yet within the family of God and even within a personal family, there can be spiritual intimidation taking place within the body of Christ. Bullying can take place from one local church to another. The apostle Paul addresses the areas that people try to use to intimidate God's people.

The area we must watch out for regarding spiritual intimidation is legalism. You may not be too familiar with legalism, but some of you are very much familiar with legalism. Legalism is simply the religion of human achievement. It is the expression of self-reliance. Legalism is the idea that somehow we can earn merit with God. Pharisees were guilty of legalism because they had come up with over six hundred rules on top of the Bible. They believed that if you obeyed all six hundred of those rules, then you were going to enter heaven.

There is another form of legalism. It's not just about our salvation and our relationship with Christ but spiritual maturity. They are making rules to define spiritual maturity. For instance, many of you know that sometimes you might go to church, and if you're not wearing certain types of clothes, they think something is wrong with you. If your hair is over your ears as a man, something is wrong with you.

Now the apostle Paul, at the outset of this verse, says, "Let no man, therefore, judge you." The word "therefore" is connecting us back to what Paul has already said. We again are reminded that our identity is not in the world; our identity is not in religion. Our identity is not in rituals, but our identity is in Jesus Christ.

That's why he says in verse 10 that you don't need anything else but Jesus Christ in your life. Understand that because we are complete in Christ, God has provided complete forgiveness. There is nothing that you can do to earn more of God's love.

I want you to know that if you judge others' spirituality and salvation by your standards that you have created, then you are violating the Scriptures. It's a sobering message; we have to recognize that legalism can intimidate people. The Bible says, "Let no man judge you."

Don't let anybody try to use standards that are human-made and do not come from the Bible to intimidate you. Saying you are not a legitimate child of God because you do not follow their human-made rules. The apostle Paul says, "Am I now seeking the approval of man or God, or am I trying to please man if so I would not be a servant of Christ."

People use legalism to intimidate others. For example, when I first showed up at The Open Door Church, a man in the church said that he was leaving the church. I said, "Why are you going to leave the church? I just got here." He said, "I'm leaving the church because your wife wears pants." Now, how crazy is that? Rather than coddle him and bow down to him, I said, "I'm going to bless and release you and pray that God sends you to a church where they believe that kind of stuff." Friends, I want you to know he was trying to use his legalism to intimidate us. He was trying to use legalism to manipulate that there are specific rules that he wants. I want to encourage every one of you to remember that we draw the line where the Bible draws the line, and where the Bible does not draw the line, we do not draw the line.

Overcoming Materialism

Someone once said, "People drive to the mall in cars that they cannot afford, to spend money that they don't have, to buy things that they don't need, to impress people that they don't like." Having a proper view of money and possessions and managing them are serious challenges that face everyone.

Sixteen of thirty-eight parables Christ told speak about how people should handle possessions and money. One out of every ten verses in the gospels talks about money. We need to think biblically about money because money matters are profoundly spiritual at their core.

Everyone needs to realize it is not a question of how much money we have; it is a question of where our heart is and what we do with what we have. If our priority is money, we will never have peace of mind.

Materialism can blind us. To overcome materialism, remember God owns everything. "The earth is the LORD's, and the fullness thereof; the world, and they that dwell therein" (Ps. 24:1 KJV). Our giving should spring from a heart that knows it owns nothing. God is looking for those who will be faithful and trustworthy to the resources He has entrusted to them.

A steward owns nothing; he is a servant who manages his master's wealth. We are managers of God's resources. "And thou say in thine heart, My power and the might of mine hand hath gotten me this wealth. But thou shalt remember the LORD thy God: for it is he that giveth thee power to get wealth, that he may establish his covenant which he sware unto thy fathers, as it is this day" (Deut. 8:17-18 KJV)

We can trust Him with our financial concerns. God provides everything. "But my God shall supply all your need according to his riches in glory by Christ Jesus" (Phil. 4:19 KJV).

Quit worrying about what we do not have. Refuse to revolve our world around money. Be content with what God gives us. "I have been young, and now am old; yet have I not seen the righteous forsaken, nor his seed begging bread" (Ps. 37:25 KJV). Material affluence does not measure God's blessings.

Materialism will fail us in the end. We can take all our stocks, bonds, and mutual fund certificates and hug them, but in the end, they will leave us cold, lonely, and in the dark.

John D. Rockefeller once said, "I have made many millions, but they have brought me no happiness."

How can you better use your money, possessions, time, and talents to serve others?

The Centrality of the Cross
1 Corinthians 1:18-23

Every great religion has a visible symbol. Buddhism: Lotus Flower; Judaism: Star of David; Islam: Crescent Moon; Christianity: Cross.

The sign of the cross identifies believers with Christ. Throughout the centuries, the Church has preserved the cross as its central symbol. Crucifixion is the cruelest method of execution known to humanity. It delayed death until they could inflict the maximum amount of torture.

Christ's death on the cross was central to His mission. "Why did you seek Me? Did you not know that I must be about My Father's business?" (Luke 2:49 NKJV). Jesus had a clear understanding of His identity and mission. God's greatest gift, and what brings Him the most glory, is His work through Jesus Christ to redeem His people. Bible scholar J. C. Ryle said, "Christ did not come on the earth to be a conqueror, or a philosopher or a mere teacher of morality. He came to save sinners."

Salvation comes through the preaching of the Word of God. The teaching of the Cross presents God's saving power. "For the preaching of the cross is to them that perish foolishness, but unto us which are saved, it is the power of God" (1 Cor. 1:18). The Greek word for "foolishness" is *mōria,* from which we get the name *moronic.* God's means of salvation is moronic in the eyes of human wisdom. But it is God's only strategy for getting the message out.[8]

Christ crucified is the only salvation for sinful men. "For I am not ashamed of the gospel of Christ: for it is the power of God unto salvation to every one that believeth; to the Jew first, and also to the Greek" (Rom. 1:16). Believe means "to trust." John uses this verb almost one hundred times in his gospel.[9]

The gospel is God's Good News regarding the salvation provided for sinful people.

Our calling is to glory in Christ and His crucifixion. "For I determined not to know anything among you, save Jesus Christ, and him crucified" (1 Cor. 2:2).

There is a story about a little girl who proudly wore a shiny cross on a chain around her neck. One day she was approached by a man who said to her, "Little girl, don't you know that the cross Jesus died on was not beautiful like the one you are wearing? It was an ugly, wooden thing." To which the girl replied, "Yes, I know. But they told me in Sunday School that whatever Jesus touches, He changes."

We should focus on the cross. "O foolish Galatians, who hath bewitched you, that ye should not obey the truth, before whose eyes Jesus Christ hath been evidently set forth, crucified among you?" (Gal 3:1). The plain preaching of a crucified Jesus is more powerful than all the oratory and philosophy of an unbelieving world.[10] Christ makes the believer wiser than the world.

---

[8] MacArthur, J. F., Jr. (1993). *Ashamed of the Gospel: When the Church becomes Like the World* (p. 114). Wheaton, IL: Crossway Books.

[9] Radmacher, E. D., Allen, R. B., & House, H. W. (1997). *The Nelson Study Bible: New King James Version* (Jn 1:7). Nashville: T. Nelson Publishers.

[10] Brooks, K. (2009). *Summarized Bible: Complete Summary of the New Testament* (p. 48). Bellingham, WA: Logos Bible Software.

Several years ago, we entertained a delightful woman in our home, Rosemaria Von Trapp, one of the famous Sound of Music children. I asked her about her parents, Captain Georg and Maria Von Trapp, who fled Nazi-occupied Austria because they refused to cooperate with the Nazis. She replied, "Only yesterday I talked to high-school students—sophomores—who were doing research papers on the Holocaust of Hitler in Germany. They wanted me to talk about the Nazis. I told them that Hitler gave us a symbol of a cross with hooks on it. But our Christian faith gives us a symbol of a cross that brings freedom and resurrection. The world, you know, offers us a glossy cross with hooks in it. My father and mother had to make a choice. They chose the cross of Christ."[11] Let us cling to the old rugged Cross, and exchange it someday for a crown.

---

[11] *More Real Stories for the Soul.* (2000). (electronic ed., pp. 291–292). Nashville: Thomas Nelson Publishers.

The Danger of Sin in Our Lives

1 Corinthians 6:12-20

Sin harms everyone involved. It gains control over those who indulge in it. Spurgeon said, "It is a great privilege not to be one's own. Does any man think it would be a pleasure to be his own? Let me assure him that there is no ruler so tyrannical as self. He that is his own master has a fool and a tyrant to be his lord."[12] It perverts God's purpose for the body. That is why we must seek what benefits everyone and stay away from people and places that will get us in trouble.

The devil wants to lead each of us into sin, and that is why we must be on guard every day. Watch out for the progression of sin. First, we associate with sin, then we tolerate sin and finally practice sin. "Blessed is the man that walketh not in the counsel of the ungodly, nor standeth in the way of sinners, nor sitteth in the seat of the scornful" (Ps. 1:1 KJV).

As Christians, we need to know what is at stake. Modern society has unleashed direct attacks against the family. Many Christians are trying to win the battle against Satan by what they do in the flesh, and consequently, they are losing the fight.

---

[12] C. H. Spurgeon, 2,200 Quotations: From the Writings of Charles H. Spurgeon : Arranged Topically or Textually and Indexed by Subject, Scripture, and People, ed. Tom Carter (Grand Rapids, MI: Baker Books, 1995), 329.

Christ gave Himself a sacrifice to redeem us from sin. God made Him sin for us, who knew no sin, that we might be made the righteousness of God in Him (2 Cor. 5:21). In this way, Christ conquers sin in us.

Only Christ can transform people into a community of the redeemed. Do not underestimate the power of the gospel. The Lord has provided all the knowledge we need to know and serve Him.

The Marks of a Mature Christian

1 Corinthians 3:1-9

Some of us never grow up—and some of us do not want to. Popular actress Gwyneth Paltrow recently expressed her frustration in that area. She said, "I have a lot of paradoxes." Paltrow continued, "Sometimes I am really assertive and decisive, and sometimes I am really nonconfrontational and indecisive. I have that duality. A lot of times, I have felt the world was too big for me, and I just wanted to go home to my parents and say, 'Take care of me,' like I'm not really grown up. I felt very confused. I went through a difficult time until things became clear. It was one of those life-altering experiences. Everything changed" (adapted from USA Weekend). Real maturity is found only in Jesus Christ.

A mature Christian is patient in their trials. We should note that the Scripture does not say if we have a trial, but it means when we have a trial. Tests are coming; there is not a person that can wake up every day and say, "My life is trouble-free." The truth is all of us have trials and problems in our lives. All of us have challenges in our lives. All of us have things that we are experiencing and we are dealing with that are very typical in our lives. We are living in times where we are facing troubling times in the world, but we must remember that we live in a flawed world.

When problems come, how do we respond? A spiritually immature person is easily upset and offended, quick to pout, quick to blame others for their problems, and must be burped often and handled with delicate gloves. We must be sure of God's purpose in our lives. God has a purpose in our lives, and God has a plan in our lives. God's overarching plan in our lives is that He would shape us into the image of the Lord Jesus Christ.

God is working in our lives and is molding our lives into the image of the Lord Jesus Christ. God is using trials in our lives; He is using tests in our lives to make us more like Jesus Christ. Therefore, we must be sure of God's purpose because it is the only way that we could be patient in our trials.

A mature Christian enjoys a balanced diet. What is a balanced diet? The milk of the Word. "As newborn babes, desire the sincere milk of the word, that ye may grow thereby" (1 Pet. 2:2 KJV). The meat of the Word. "For when for the time ye ought to be teachers, ye have need that one teach you again which be the first principles of the oracles of God; and are become such as have need of milk, and not of strong meat. For every one that useth milk is unskillful in the word of righteousness: for he is a babe. But strong meat belongeth to them that are of full age, even those who by reason of use have their senses exercised to discern both good and evil" (Heb. 5:12-14 KJV).

A mature Christian knows how to get along with others. Refuse to harbor anger in our lives. Never put others down because we disagree with them. Confess our sins of jealousy and strife. Pray for those we disagree with. Do something for those we disagree with. Put others first.

A mature Christian seeks to glorify God rather than people. How do we glorify God? Focus on Christ, not people or problems. See ministers as instruments, not the source of salvation. Give God credit for any success or increase.

Desires to be a team player. How to be a team player? We need each other. We all have a job to do. Our reward is in heaven. Be cooperative. It is about Him.

While many of us have seen pictures of a huge eagle's nest high in the branches of a tree or in a cliff, few of us have gotten a glimpse inside. When a mother eagle builds her nest, she starts with thorns, broken branches, sharp rocks, and several other items that seem entirely unsuitable for the project. However, then she lines the nest with a thick padding of wool, feathers, and fur from animals she has killed, making it soft and comfortable for the eggs. By the time the growing birds reach flying age, the comfort of the nest and the luxury of free meals make them quite reluctant to leave. That is when the mother eagle begins "stirring up the nest." With her sharp talons, she begins pulling up the thick carpet of fur and feathers, bringing the sharp rocks and branches to the surface. As more of the bedding gets plucked up, the nest becomes more uncomfortable for the young eagles. Eventually, this and other urgings prompt the growing eagles to leave their once-comfortable abode and move on to more mature behavior. So it is with God through the circumstances of life; He is moving each of us to more mature behavior.

Three Guidelines on Making Judgments
Matthew 7:1-6

We often hear people say, "The Bible says, 'Do not judge others.'" A press release from Barna stated that, in the 2007 survey, "just 16% of non-Christians in their late teens and twenties said they have a 'good impression' of Christianity." Among young non-Christians, Barna said, most of the perceptions of Christianity were negative, such as that Christianity is judgmental (87%). Even young Christians are being affected: half said they perceived their faith to be judgmental.

However, the Bible does teach us to judge others. Jesus said, "You will know them by their fruits." The ability to make judgments about people and circumstances is essential to safety and protection. God never instructs us not to carry out judgments, but instead, He gives us guidelines on how to make judgments. In Matthew Chapter 7, Jesus lays out for us three guidelines for judgments.

GUIDELINE #1: BE CAUTIOUS

Jesus teaches us not to rush into a judgment of people and circumstances. The reason we should be cautious about our judgments is that God will judge us one day. Before we decide, we need to examine ourselves and make sure that we are not as guilty as those we want to judge. We do not have much right to complain about the mistakes made by people who are doing the work we should be doing. "Therefore you are inexcusable, O man, whoever you are who judge, for in whatever you judge another you condemn yourself; for you who judge practice the same things" (Rom. 2:1 NKJV).

The second reason we should not be quick to judge others is that we are not God. We tend to think that we know everything about the matter. The truth is that we do not know all the circumstances or the facts. We need to be more cautious about our judgments until we have learned more about the truth. It is much easier to be critical than correct.

Ultimately, only God is qualified to judge correctly because of His infinite knowledge. Thus, sometimes we may have to leave the matter and judgment into His hands.

GUIDELINE #2: BE COMPASSIONATE

The problem that Jesus was addressing in the gospel of Matthew was a group of people who were arrogant and self-righteous. Unfortunately, people do try to act superior to others. Nevertheless, the ground is level at the foot of the cross!

We all have failures and weaknesses that we need to remember when we are judging others. Instead of focusing on the little specks of dust in other people's eyes, we should take care of the beam in our eye. The greatest of all faults is to imagine that we have none.

Jesus also reminds us that whatever we use to measure someone's life and actions, that same measure will apply to us. Therefore, because we want to be judged mercifully by our peers and God, we will, in turn, do our best to judge others with compassion. Remember, we are not put on this earth to see through one another, but to see one another through.

GUIDELINE #3: BE COURAGEOUS

Being courageous in our judgments means first examining ourselves. When we are honest and humble, then we can face up to our problems and weaknesses and confess them to God. Once we have cleared up our issues, which might take some time, then we can see clearly to make proper judgments.

Jesus warns us about having enough discernment to accurately judge a person or circumstance, not to cast pearls before swine. That means we have to be courageous enough to look within and without. Often, we depend on others who should not be trusted, and they trample our pearl of trust. Often, we cast before people the pearls of our heart, and it is taken advantage of or abused. We must train ourselves, and our children, to not be naive but to be courageous in our judgment and discernment.

Four Keys to Effective Evangelism and Missions through the Church

Acts 5:12-42

The Church has an assignment and responsibility for gathering in and sending out. We cannot ignore this calling as a Church as we present the gospel's message of hope.

One of the highest calling for a Christian is to be a witness for Jesus. For the Church to be effective in evangelizing the community and the world, four keys must be correct in the Church.

First, the Church must remain pure. In the book of Acts chapter 5, the apostle Peter confronts the sinful deceit of Ananias and Sapphira. The result was a sweeping Godly fear within the Church and without. This purity only validated the life-changing message of the gospel.

Whether it is personally or corporately, there are three ingredients that help us remain pure: accountability, scripture, and prayer.

Second, the Church must be an instrument of God's power. We learn from the book of Acts That The Secret To The Church's Effectiveness Is Having God's Power Upon Them.

How can we be an instrument of His power?

Be faithful. Be faithful to Him who has called us and to the work He has called us. God is looking for servants who will be reliable. When He finds them, He pours out His power upon them. God is not looking for great ability but dependability.

If We Will Have Our Tools Ready, Then God Will Find Us Work And Empower Us To Do That Work.

Thirdly, we must prepare the Church for Satanic persecution. When God Blesses A Church, And People Are Saved, And Lives Are Changed, Then Satan Will Not Be Happy. Every servant of God will face challenges.

"Beloved, do not be surprised at the fiery trial when it comes upon you to test you, as though something strange were happening to you" (1 Pet. 4:12 ESV).

Those whom Satan will use to discourage us are the religious people all around you. These religious people will call you names and frown upon your zeal. Yet Be Not Discouraged, Because, Through Persecution, God Is Validating His Approval Upon Us. Not Everyone Will Like You When You Are Passionate About Missions And Evangelism, But That's OK Because God Is Smiling Down From Heaven Upon Us.

Finally, the Church must be persistent in the face of opposition. When we face opposition to advancing the kingdom of God, It Is Important To Remain Obedient To God. The Early Church Publicly Demonstrated Its Allegiance To God By Refusing To Obey Men And Choosing To Obey God.

God may be calling us to a higher life in missions through giving and going. However, our family and friends may be trying to discourage us. Only listen to the voice of God because where He guides, He will provide.

Faithfulness

> "And let us consider one another in order to stir up
> love and good works, not forsaking the assembling
> of ourselves together, as is the manner of some,
> but exhorting one another, and so much the more
> as you see the Day approaching"
> (Heb. 10:24-25 NKJV).

What does it mean to be faithful? The root meaning of faithfulness (Heb. ›emunah) is "certainty" and "dependability."

Today we should resolve to be faithful to the church services. We cast our vote to close that service when we choose not to attend. We need the church. Our church needs us. The church is a community of people who voluntarily enter into a relationship with one another to accomplish kingdom goals. It is a place where we minister and receive ministry.

We need to be obedient to our Lord and Savior who bled and died to purchase the Church with His precious blood. We also need to be faithful to keep the covenant we made to our church when we joined. Most church covenants state that members will support their church family through constant attendance.

Someone once asked a pastor to define "faithful attendance at worship," and this was his reply:

All that we ask is that we apply the same standards of faithfulness to our church activities that we would in other areas of our lives. That does not seem too much to ask. The church, after all, is concerned about faithfulness.

Consider these examples: If our car started one out of three times, would we consider it faithful? If the paperboy skipped Mondays and Thursdays, would they be missed? If we did not show up at work two or three times a month, would our boss call us faithful? If our refrigerator quit a day now and then, would we excuse it and say, "Oh well, it works most of the time"? If our water heater greets us with cold water one or two mornings a week while we were in the shower, would it be faithful? If we miss a couple of mortgage payments in a year's time, would your mortgage holder say, "Oh well, ten out of twelve is not bad"? If we miss worship and attend meetings only often enough to show we are interested but not often enough to get involved, are we faithful?

The Marine Corps has a compelling motto, Semper Fidelis; the short is Semper Fi. Perhaps we have seen that on windows or bumpers of cars. Semper Fidelis are two Latin words that mean "Always Faithful." It is the code of conduct and character of the gallant soldiers of the Corps. It is a description of their loyalty and a definition of their lives as Marines. It is supposed to be their driven purpose as honorable and dedicated soldiers to this branch of service—Always Faithful.

May it be said of God's people. Always Faithful.

Be a Peacemaker Not a Troublemaker

James 4:1-7

The mark of a mature Christian is to be a peacemaker and not a troublemaker. When we come to James chapter 4, that is precisely the situation that James is dealing with in verse 1: "Where do wars and fights come from among you..." There was conflict within the church, and he is challenging God's people to be peacemakers rather than troublemakers.

Our calling is to be peacemakers. God commands us in two different ways to be peacemakers. First and foremost, to make peace with God. We need to get our hearts right with the Lord. Then we need to make peace with one another. James mainly is focusing on us getting things right with God because he knows that at the heart of all conflict is pride. James does not want there to be conflict because he knows a battle is not God's will for the Church, but instead, He wants there to be peace. He wants God's people to work hard at making peace. Now the devil always tries to lead us astray, and he is "...a roaring lion seeking whom he may devour..." He's still trying to cause problems with others and is always working to cause issues in our relationship with our Savior.

We come to verse six, and this is where we are to focus on making peace with God and to restore our relationship with God. What I find so interesting in this passage is that James is not worried about offending people. He's already boldly calling them adulterers in the sense that they are practicing spiritual unfaithfulness to God. The apostle doesn't shrink back from the role and responsibility of telling God's truth. The beautiful thing about James is he does not leave us hanging with condemnation but admonishes us to get our hearts right with Jesus. He says, "Let me help you get right with God and to follow what Jesus requires of us." It is always God's plan that God's people would be victorious over the world, the flesh, and the devil.

Remember, the Scriptures teach us, "...we are more than conquerors..." The Bible teaches us that we are to live a victorious Christian life. James lays out for us a cure for worldliness in our hearts. The ordained way is that we are to receive God's grace. The Bible says in James 4:6, "...that he gives more grace. Therefore, he says God resists the proud but gives grace to the humble." Underscore two phrases, "...he gives more grace..." and "...he gives grace to the humble." These words are essential at the outset if we are going to come back to God that we receive His grace. These are sweet words in the Scriptures. They are to bring great peace to our hearts to know that God is offering us His mercy. Every believer is a particular object of God's grace. Think about the beautiful truth that the grace of God saves us. The Bible teaches us, "For by grace are you saved through faith that not of yourselves it is a gift of God not of works lest any man should boast." Here is a beautiful truth: not only do I need grace for salvation, but I need grace for every day in my life. The grace of Jesus is never exhausted.

When you and I need grace in our trials, He gives grace. When we need grace for our struggles, He pours more grace into our lives. Even when we need grace for our tongue, and we need forgiveness for making things right with God and grace for making things right with others, He gives more grace. God does not just say, "I want to provide you with enough grace to give you salvation, and then I'm going to leave you on your own."

God understands that you and I are wrestling with the flesh, the devil, and the world, and therefore we are in much need of this inexhaustible grace that He makes available to us. Let us not forget that we are not only saved by grace, but each of us as believers live by grace. Many Christians are failing in their life because they are not asking, nor are they receiving the grace of God daily in their life. Because of that, they are living their lives in the flesh. The world and the devil himself are influencing them, and thus they are not living a godly life but a worldly life. God is saying, "I will pour more grace upon the humble."

Patient in Trials & Temptations

James 5:1-8

Each chapter in the book of James has a different mark of a mature Christian. Now what James does in chapters 1 through 5, he gives us the marks of a mature Christian. Then he begins to explain how we can achieve those marks in our Christian life. In chapter 1, we learn how to be patient in our trials.

One time, a lady asked me, "Pastor, should I pray for patience? I heard that I should not pray for patience, is that right?" I said, "Well, whether you like it or not, you're going to have to deal with problems, and God wants us to be patient." When we think of patience in our trials, we're thinking about endurance. We're not just saying that we're tolerant but that we are enduring, persevering, and remaining steadfast in our faith for the Lord Jesus Christ. No matter what the trials are, we continue to be faithful to our Lord and Savior Jesus.

To help us to be patient, we must be sure of God's purpose in our lives. In James chapter 1 and verse 4, go back quickly because I do not want you to forget it. At the outset, he says, "Let patience have its perfect or maturing work that you may be perfect or mature and complete lacking nothing."

God's purpose for your life is that you would be like Jesus. Our calling is to bring glory to God and to be like the Lord Jesus Christ. God uses circumstances, problems, trials, and tribulations in my life to perfect me, to mature me, and to help me grow in my faith.

Therefore, it's my response to those trials based upon what I know that helps me to demonstrate patience. So much that James says in verse 3 is not how I feel. It's what I know that helps me to endure for the Lord Jesus Christ. We cannot forget that we must continue to grow in that and understand that.

The second saying is that if we're going to be patient in our trials, we must be sure of God's goodness. Look at verse 17, what James is trying to communicate to us about us being patient. He says, "Every good gift and every perfect gift is from above and comes down from the father of lights whom there is no variation or shadow of turning."

James wants us to know that our God is good. Remember that when we have a trial, the first thing that comes to our mind and our heart is the question of why. Many times, if we are not rooted in our faith, and growing in our walk with the Lord Jesus Christ, there will be a tendency in our human nature to become angry toward God. I have met many people who are mad toward God because of their circumstances, and they are distraught with God.

I remember as a young pastor serving in Indiana, I was only in my twenties pastoring a church. The local funeral director called me and said, "Pastor, a young mother has lost her baby. Would you come down and talk to her? She doesn't have a pastor; she doesn't have a church." I said, "Certainly!"

I took off, went down to the funeral home. As soon as I walked into the room and began to try to console her, she looked up at me and said, "Don't give me that God stuff." I understand in the sense, not that I've been there, but I know that her heart is hurting, and she is struggling with hope. There's a tremendous sense of anger in her heart.

That can happen to the believer if we do not get back to the full assurance and confidence that our God is good. We understand that He is right. The Psalmist said, "Thou are good and do good."

When we think about the goodness of God, we must remember that by nature, God is good. Which means He is morally excellent, extraordinarily beautiful, and extravagantly bountiful. The Bible says, "Oh, give thanks unto the Lord, for he is good for his mercy endures forever."

The goodness of God is crucial in your life. Therefore, the apostle Paul took so much time in his letters to teach doctrine first. Then as the principle was the foundation of the Christian faith, he brought in the application. No application can supersede the foundation of the doctrine of who God is.

We must understand that as we walk through trials, grasping the goodness of God is crucial to us in how we respond in patience as a result of our trials and tribulations in our lives. God is good. He is the essence of goodness. It does not mean that He is just the greatest, but rather that He is in Himself the best. He is excellent; He is a good God.

Now James goes on to describe not only the goodness of God in verse 17, but did you notice, at the end, there is no variation or shadow of turning? He helps us understand that God is immutable, which means that God does not change. I must know this when I'm walking through a trial.

My God is good. He is kind toward me, and not only is He good, but His goodness and who He is will never change. God is the same today, tomorrow, and forever. The Scriptures teach us that who God is yesterday, He is today and will be tomorrow. My circumstances may change, but God will never change.

So when I declared that God was good yesterday and the sun was shining and my car was working and the bank was full and I had a job with friends, that same God is good tomorrow when my boss fires me. The same God is good when the clouds gather round and it rains all day. We must remember that our expression and declaration and praise of the goodness of God is not just when our circumstances are exceptional.

It is essential in all of our Christian life that we declare and praise His goodness even when our circumstances are continually changing, and even when we struggle. My conditions do not modify the character of God. At the foundation of what I know and believe as a follower of Christ is that my God is good, and His goodness will not change. Therefore, it is the goodness of God that becomes a source of strength and sustaining power in my life.

As I walk through trials in my life, anything short of that, any belief system that does not put its confidence in who God is, is going to crumble. Life is going to lead you on a roller coaster, and you are going to be continually struggling. It is the goodness of God that should lead us to be a people who not only praise God but a people who repent. Some of you who are hearing the gospel today need to come to the Lamb of God, who can take away your sins.

The Mission of the Church

Matthew 28:16-20

Our mission is to make disciples. "Go, therefore, and make disciples of all the nations" (Matt. 28:19 NKJV). Tragically many Christians are unwilling to fulfill this mission. Unfortunately, many Christians think little about their mission.

God calls us to bring a message of hope to people whom we meet daily. Christ has commanded us as believers to make disciples. Therefore, we should willingly submit to His authority. "All authority has been given to Me in heaven and on earth" (Matt. 28:18 NKJV).

Discipleship is the birth and growth of a believer by which we become more like Christ every day. "The word of God kept on spreading, and the number of the disciples continued to increase greatly in Jerusalem, and a great many of the priests were becoming obedient to the faith" (Acts 6:7 NASB).

If we are to fulfill this command, we must go to people. "And he said unto them, Go ye into all the world, and preach the gospel to every creature" (Mark 16:15 KJV). Heaven's agenda is the great commission. "For the Son of man is come to seek and to save that which was lost" (Luke 19:10 KJV). Evangelism is the number one priority for the Church.

It's exciting to see people come to know Christ as Savior. There's only one way to God—through Jesus. Every believer is responsible for sharing the good news. "As you sent me into the world, so I have sent them into the world" (John 17:18 ESV)

A church is a hospital for sinners and not a country club for the saints. Christians have good news to tell the world. When Dr. Adrian Rogers was once asked, "When is a church big enough?" He replied, "When everyone on the planet knows Jesus."

<u>How can we reach the lost?</u>

Pray for the lost. "Therefore, pray earnestly to the Lord of the harvest to send out laborers into his harvest" (Matt. 9:38 ESV). Memorize scripture; build friendships with the lost; be trained to share the gospel. "But sanctify the Lord God in your hearts: and be ready always to give an answer to every man that asketh you a reason of the hope that is in you with meekness and fear" (1 Pet. 3:15 KJV). Who are you bringing to Christ?

<u>We've a story to tell to the nations,</u>
We've a story to tell to the nations,
That shall turn their hearts to the right,
A story of truth and mercy,
A story of peace and light,
A story of peace and light.

About the Author

Mike hosts the weekly television program called "Hope Worth Having. It airs on Master Media (check HopeWorthHaving.com for local listings). Hope Worth Having airs on Sunday mornings at 11:30 a.m. on WLYH Lighthouse 49 (Chambersburg, PA, Cable Channel 18; Carlisle/Gettysburg, PA, Cable Channel 21; Ephrata, PA, Cable Channel 8; Harrisburg/York, PA, Cable Channel 7; Hershey, PA, Cable Channel 13; Lancaster/Lebanon, PA, Cable Channel 10; Direct TV Channel 49; Dish Channel 49; Verizon Fios Channel 17). It also airs on Thursdays 10:00 p.m. WLYH Lighthouse 49 in PA and on Fridays at 10:00 a.m. on Atlanta 57 in GA. You can also view Hope Worth Having every Sunday morning Live Stream by visiting www.hopeworthhaving.com at 10:30 a.m.

He is the voice of the "Hope Worth Having" radio programs. The Hope Worth Having radio program airs Friday at 4:30 p.m. in Wilkes-Barre/Scranton, PA–WITK AM 1550; Saturday at 1:00 p.m. in Wilkes-Barre/Scranton, PA–WITK AM 1550; Saturday at 5:00 p.m. in York, PA–WYYC AM 1250; Sunday 9:00 a.m. in Alabama and Georgia–WPIL 91.7; Sunday 9:30 a.m. McConnellsburg, PA–WEEO FM 103.7; Sunday 9:30 a.m. York, PA–WYYC AM 1250; Sunday 10:30 a.m. Pittsburgh, PA–WWNL AM 1080; Sunday 10:30 a.m. Sweetwater, TN–WDEH AM 800; Tuesday 2:00 p.m. in Alabama and Georgia–WPIL 91.7; Thursday 11:00 a.m. in Alabama and Georgia–WPIL 97.7.

In addition, Mike serves as the President of Cumberland Valley Christian School, helping a new generation of students prepare for God's purpose for their lives.

He is the former Chairman of the Trustee Board at Davis College in Binghamton, New York. Davis is a fully accredited Bible college training young people to effectively serve God in America and around the world.

Pastor Sanders holds a BA in Pastoral Theology and an MA in Biblical Studies.

CPSIA information can be obtained
at www.ICGtesting.com
Printed in the USA
BVHW050551140721
611528BV00007B/102